100
Things
Every Adult College Student
Ought to Know

A self-orientation guide with definitions, customs, procedures,
and advice to assist adults in adjusting to the start of college.

by Carlette Jackson Hardin

Cambridge Stratford Study Skills Institute
Williamsville, NY

100 Things Every Adult College Student Ought to Know
by Carlette Jackson Hardin

Copyright © 2000
The Cambridge Stratford Study Skills Institute
A division of Cambridge Stratford, Ltd.
8560 Main Street, Williamsville, New York 14221.
For information: (716) 626-9044.

Library of Congress Number: 99-76786
ISBN: 0-935637-26-5   Printed in the USA
Printing is the lowest number: 10 9 8 7 6   *Drawings by Ellen Klem*

Introduction

If you are reading this book, you are probably an adult student who has recently returned to college, or you are an adult who is considering entering college. If you haven't been on a college campus lately, you may not know that what was once considered the typical college student has changed drastically. The typical college student is no longer a traditional eighteen-year-old who leaves his/her parents and moves into the college dorm. While such students can still be found on college campuses, they have been joined by baby boomers who have decided to enter college for the first time or to reenter after an extended absence from academic life.

Sitting in class beside teenagers with spiked hair and nose rings, are gray-haired grandmothers. On the intramural fields are teams of forty-year-olds playing against teams from fraternity row.

Upwards of 50% of students on many college campuses today are over the age of twenty-five! These adult learners bring experiences to the classroom that add to the wealth of information available to all students. Adult students are described by their instructors as more eager, motivated and committed than traditionally aged students. Adult students do well in their classes and usually set the curve in most courses. They bring to campus tremendous strengths: their strong desire to learn, their ability to relate their new learning to what they already know, and their ability to use their prior experience to find answers to questions that confuse or concern them. Yet, most adult students find that starting college can be filled with confusion. This book can bring clarity.

Unfortunately, traditional age students do have some advantages. Because they have had more recent experiences in the classroom, they often have a better understanding of the rules, regulations and customs of higher education. This lack of knowledge often creates barriers that adult students find hard to overcome. Often, adult students find they don't know where to go for information and because many leave campus as soon as classes end, they may never establish a network of classmates to provide this key information. Therefore, adult students find everything from the vocabulary to the administrative structure of the academic environment new and foreign. When adult students lack this information about critical aspects of college, they may hesitate to go back to school or, they drop out because they don't know where to go for assistance. Thus, the purpose of *100 Things Every Adult College Student Ought to Know* is to equip adult students with the knowledge to make a smoother adjustment to their entry or reentry to college.

The information for this book was obtained by asking hundreds of adult students, just like you, what they felt were the most important things adult students needed to know. They told me that adult students need a way to maneuver around the maze of terms and vocabulary used on a college campus. Others suggested that adult students needed information so that they could successfully balance their roles of parent, spouse, employee, and student. Some asked for information that would help them become a better student. Additionally, instructors with experience teaching adult learners were asked what things they believed adult learners ought to know. Their comments shed further light on their understanding of the double, triple, or quadruple roles adult learners must balance to be successful in their academic lives.

Six chapters were developed from the data and suggestions collected. The first chapter, "Getting Started," provides information about what a student needs to know before enrolling in college. It is designed to help the adult learner find the best college to fit his/her needs. Also, if planning to transfer in the future, this section may set broad parameters for researching the best choices. The second chapter, "Understanding the Definitions and Customs," highlights some of the unique practices, customs, and definitions used commonly in higher education. It's tied to a convenient glossary listed in the back of the book that should help build your vocabulary so you can communicate better with campus officials and professors. The third chapter, "Knowing the Turf, Rules, and Players," provides a way of thinking and acting in college. It is based on information that former adult students felt you should know to help you avoid the pitfalls commonly associated with making the adjustment to the start of college. It will require some thinking and soul searching on your part regarding your individual needs. However, it should be worth the effort as its concluding theme implies: "Getting off to a right start will be your best investment in meeting your goals and dreams." The fourth chapter, "Reaching Out," outlines what many students who rush home each day after classes never discover, namely the wealth of services that are available to you beyond the classroom. It also covers some important "do's" for avoiding some of the problems faced by adult students. The fifth chapter, "Putting First Things First," outlines how to deal with our prime concerns: our existing family and friends and the new network of people who will mold our futures. This chapter is one of the primary reasons why the first term or semester "will be tough." The sixth chapter, "Studying Smart," offers proven steps that you can take to increase your success. It provides a road map of immediate directions adult students have found to work and opens key topics that can lead you to a wealth of helpful information. A glossary and alphabetical index are also provided at the end to assist you in quickly locating information by topical headings.

I wish to thank the hundreds of adult students who shared their thoughts and insights. A special thanks to Mira Fleschman (Nashville State Technical Institue) and Ken Stanley who reviewed the final version and gave their suggestions as to how it could better meet the needs of community college and male students. Also, thanks to one of the authorities in the field, Louis Vangieri (Sound Behavior, Training & Consulting), for suggesting and offering excerpts from his training materials that proved valuable and to Lauren Bachner-Vangieri for filling in gaps and faculty perspectives.

I hope this little book makes more than a little impact on your successful adaptation and transition to college. Read it, review it often, and carry it with you during your first term at college. It will become a resource you can use to help navigate your clear path and will provide key tips you can share with family, friends, and college personnel to get the help you need to accomplish your academic goals. Although *100 Things* is used in the title, there are more than 100 items. I would love to have 100 more for our next edition. I welcome your reactions and comments. An Editorial Contribution form is attached at the end. Please share your comments so others beginning college in the future can learn from your experiences. Happy reading and good luck as you begin your academic adventure.

Dr. Carlette Jackson Hardin

Dr. Carlette Jackson Hardin is a Professor of Education at Austin Peay State University in Clarksville, Tennessee. During her eighteen year career in higher education, Dr. Hardin has worked extensively with adult students as an advisor, workshop leader, and sponsor of support groups for returning students. Through these interactions, she has learned of the needs, concerns, fears, and goals of adult students. She provides information concerning effective programing and teaching for the adult learner in presentations, inservices, and workshops across the country. Former president of the National Association for Developmental Education, Dr. Hardin strives to meet the needs of all at-risk students.

Table of Contents

<table>
<tr><td>

1

</td><td>

Getting Started

College is not just for the creative or the really smart people. It is for ordinary folks who want to improve their lives.

</td></tr>
</table>

Michael, 42 years old
English Major

Adult College Students Ought to Know:

1.   that **it's never too** late to follow a dream. If you have always dreamed of going to college or returning to college, it's time to start. In fact, in 1995 there were 6.1 million* adult students who were following their dreams by being in college. It is estimated that by the year 2007 the number will have increased to 6.4 million. Go for it! You won't be alone.

* National Center for Education Statistics–1999

Adult College Students Ought to Know:

2.   that there is **no need for guilt**. Understand that you are seeking to improve your situation through education. The best gift you can give yourself or your family is an education. When you receive your diploma, most everyone will agree the sacrifices made by you and your family were worth the effort.

Adult College Students Ought to Know:

3.   that it won't help to dwell on what **you should have learned** 10-20 years ago. You can't turn back the clock, but you can make up for lost time. Don't dwell on the past. Determine that starting today you are going to absorb as much knowledge as you can.

Adult College Students Ought to Know:

4.   that **past academic records can be erased**. Many adults returning to college may have started as traditional students. However, some may have dropped out due to financial obligations, competing responsibilities, or lack of focus, motivation, and maturity. "I dreaded revealing my grades from my last institution," stated one student. "Then I realized many colleges offer programs to clear up past performances and start fresh." While different terms are used by different institutions, most offer opportunities to make up or erase past academic difficulties. With a clear attitude, a clean slate can get you re-started on the right path.

Adult College Students Ought to Know:

5. that **many institutions provide specialized programs** and trained personnel to work with adult learner needs. Many community colleges that have historically served adult learners have programs and personnel that effectively serve both traditional and non-traditional students. Four-year institutions often dedicate specially trained individuals to handle the needs of adult learners—admission counselors, advisers, financial aid counselors, and coordinators of support programs and special services. These are designed for your specific needs. Seek out these resources to ease your transition at the start of college.

Adult College Students Ought to Know:

6.   that **you are self-motivated**. You aren't seeking a degree because it is what is expected or what your parents want you to do. You are seeking a degree because you have decided that this is what you need to do to have the best life possible for you and your family. You are eager to learn, and that means you will be willing to do the work, ask for assistance, and stretch your limits.

Adult College Students Ought to Know:

7.   that you are **more well-rounded and at ease with people** than traditional age students. Being older, you have had more experiences in life, and these experiences will serve you well as you pursue your degree. You've met more people and been to more places. You will be able to interact more easily with others (even professors). As you go further in your academic career, your life experiences will serve you well.

Adult College Students Ought to Know:

8.   that many **adult students initially enroll as "Non-Degree Students."** Therefore, if you aren't sure if you want to enroll as a degree seeking student or if you aren't sure you want to do more than just take a few classes for personal growth, find out if the option of being a "non-degree student" is available to you. Typically, colleges allow adult students who have a high school diploma, but who haven't attended college previously, to register for up to 12 hours before being formally admitted. [NOTE: If eligible for financial aid, request advice about this option.]

Adult College Students Ought to Know:

9.   that many students can attend college without **ever step-
ping foot on a college campus**. More and more colleges
are bringing courses to students. College courses are offered at
churches, schools, community centers, the work site, etc. Check
with your employer to see what opportunities are available to
you. In fact, some employers reimburse students for course
completion with a passing grade.

Not only are these courses offered at locations that are convenient, they are often offered at times that allow you to continue with your normal schedule. In addition, many courses are now available via distance learning on TV satellite, the internet, or through correspondence courses. Distance learning is a viable life-long learning option for many professional and other adult students. In addition, a course reduction may be available for distance learning courses as compared to the same credit earned through on-campus completion. Check with your campus to see what's available.

Adult College Students Ought to Know:

10. that attending **evening classes** can be an ideal way to balance work, family, friends, and college. You can reserve time before class to unwind, catch up on reading, and prepare for class. After class, a quick trip to the library can help you finish homework, review your notes, or prepare for tests.

Adult College Students Ought to Know:

11. that **entry into college can be a gradual process**. You don't have to take a full load the first term you attend. Take one course and see how you feel about being in an academic environment. If you are comfortable and successful, you can increase your load the next term.

If you decide to go full-time your first term, don't take too many classes as an effort to make up for lost time. You have taken the right step by getting started, but be realistic. You can't make up for the years you lost by loading on extra hours. Enroll for the hours you can handle while balancing your family and other responsibilities. It may take a little longer, but the result will be better mental health for you, better relationships with those you love, and better grades overall.

Adult College Students Ought to Know:

12. that you can **audit courses**. Auditing is like being a listener in a course and receiving no grade. If you are nervous about taking that first course, you might want to audit a course. While payment is usually required, auditing allows you to take a course without the worry of earning a grade. This is a chance to test the waters. Also, a pass/fail grade is an option in some courses. This allows you to complete course requirements without worrying about an "A", "C, " etc. Many colleges have restrictions on when you can audit a course and/or if courses are offered with the pass/fail option, so check with your college regarding its policy.

Adult College Students Ought to Know:

13. that many campuses hold **special orientation sessions** for adult students. Attend! These sessions will provide valuable information about the campus. You will have a chance to meet other adult students who are going through the same struggles and challenges as you. Many times such sessions offer an opportunity for students to register for classes in a more relaxed atmosphere and meet professors who can provide details and help.

Adult College Students Ought to Know:

14. that you have **several choices in choosing** a post-secondary institution. Institutions fall into one of four types, each with advantages and disadvantages. Your individual needs, circumstances, and educational requirements will assist you in deciding which is best for you. The four types are:

a.   Two-Year Colleges – Sometimes called community colleges, these schools tend to emphasize specialized vocational, pre-professional, job-oriented courses. Many offer two-year liberal arts programs transferable to four-year institutions. Two-year community colleges typically have a slightly older student body, and they cater to the needs of these students by providing many courses on nights and weekends. They are often less expensive than four-year colleges. In addition, classes tend to be smaller at two-year schools.

b.   Public colleges and universities – Because these institutions receive public funding, they provide quality education at reasonable prices. A variety of majors are offered. However, not all majors are offered at all institutions, so be sure to ask about the major you desire.

c.   Private college and universities – Some of these institutions carry more prestige than public institutions, but also carry higher tuition fees. They often emphasize quality education that meets individualized needs with smaller classes and specialized majors.

d.   Technical and vocational schools – These schools offer specialized training in a variety of fields. The emphasis is on job training. If your desire is to enter the job market quickly, a vocational diploma may serve you well. If your desire is to have a career that allows you more upward mobility, a more traditional degree may be what you want.

Adult College Students Ought to Know:

15. that not all institutions are **accredited**. Therefore, the coursework at these institutions is not recognized by some companies or acceptable for transfer to other institutions. Be sure to ask about the type of accreditation of the institution and the transferability of the coursework to other institutions.

Adult College Students Ought to Know:

16. that many colleges give **credit for life experiences and credit by examination**. You may be eligible for degree credit for previous work experience or other activities. This is sometimes called life experience credit. You may earn credit based on your performance on specified examinations. These exams can be the college's own challenge examinations or those of the College-Level Examination Program (CLEP). Discuss these options with your admissions counselor. The experiences you've had before attending college may speed your goal of earning a degree. [NOTE: Credit received may not count toward your Grade Point Average and may not be transferable to another college.]

Adult College Students Ought to Know:

17. that many institutions allow students to create "**adult student degrees**." By putting together credits earned by life experiences, testing, military experience, and credit from other institutions, a degree unique to the student is created. This "degree by design" can meet the unique needs of an adult student.

Adult College Students Ought to Know:

18. that every institution **publishes a catalog** of its academic programs, policies, procedures, and course descriptions. These catalogs are also called bulletins at some institutions. Before enrolling at any institution, request a catalog. Check admissions policies. Find out about the accreditation of the institution. Learn if the institution has the major you want, or if not, prepares you to transfer to an institution that does.

Once you enroll, keep the catalog. Unless an external, outside accrediting or licensing group changes a requirement that forces a change in your program, most institutions allow you to graduate under the requirements listed in the catalog in place when you entered. A curriculum checksheet is often available listing all requirements needed to attain your degree. Get one early. While there is typically a time limit on how long one has to complete a degree under a specific catalog, this policy will protect you if for some reason you must take a leave from school.

If you leave the institution, keep the catalog. If you decide to transfer later, the catalog may serve as a record of the courses you took in helping the new institution grant transfer credit.

Adult College Students Ought to Know:

19. that you will be welcomed to join the ranks of student learners and will be identified as a special participant. **Many different titles are used**. You may be called "adult learners," "non-traditional students," "mature students," "returning students," "older students," or "adult students." Whatever the title, these students are defined as often juggling many different roles and responsibilities with work, family, or community commitments. Like you, they are electing to juggle into their mix of responsibilities, the role of college student. This is an act of a highly motivated person. You should be as proud to join their ranks as colleges are to have you bring your valuable experience to share with other students in each classroom.

Activity 1
Selecting the Right School for You

List two or three schools you are considering attending. For each
item, check if the school meets your needs.

Needs	School One	School Two	School Three
Convenient to work and home	_____	_____	_____
Courses offered at convenient times	_____	_____	_____
Offers degree I want to earn	_____	_____	_____

Needs	School One	School Two	School Three
Offers option to remove past records	_____	_____	_____
Allows students to enroll as "non-degree"	_____	_____	_____
Provides option to audit courses	_____	_____	_____
Courses available			
Where I work	_____	_____	_____
Via Internet	_____	_____	_____
Via TV	_____	_____	_____

Needs	School One	School Two	School Three
Provides services for adult students	_____	_____	_____
Is accredited	_____	_____	_____
Accepts credit for			
Life Experiences	_____	_____	_____
Military Credit	_____	_____	_____
Testing	_____	_____	_____

Based on the above assessment, where would you enroll?

_____

No goal is unattainable.

Adult students are often confused by the jargon of academic life.

2

Understanding the Definitions and Customs

Adult students ought to know that being homecoming queen is not an option.

Marla
35 year old Sophomore

Adult College Students Ought to Know:

20. that each **campus has its own list of definitions and terms**. You may be asked to give your PIN (Personal Identification Number) or your SID (Student Identification Number). Don't be afraid to ask what a term means. It may save you time and frustration if you do. A glossary of the most common terms used on campuses appears at the end of this book. Review it. You'll begin to feel more comfortable when you can use these terms in your discussions with faculty, staff, and fellow students.

Adult College Students Ought to Know:

21. that you will use a **student identification number** every time you do anything official with the institution. Many institutions use a student's social security number for this purpose. Other institutions provide this number for students. Be sure to learn this number (or carry it with you).

Adult College Students Ought to Know:

22. that the **definition of an academic year** varies from institution to institution. The typical year begins with the opening of classes each August or September through final examinations and graduation in the spring. Commonly, the academic year consists of two semesters or three quarters, followed by an additional summer session (with possible short intercessions) of course offerings. Your college catalog or bulletin will provide these dates.

Adult College Students Ought to Know:

23. the **importance of having an Academic Advisor**. The academic advisor is usually a faculty or staff member who advises the student about his or her academic program. However, advisors serve a much more important function than simply signing your course request form. Besides being able to advise you of what specific courses you must take, they know all about your major and the requirements for graduation. They know other professors and can direct you to professors who will match your learning style. They can help find internships and serve as a reference when you apply for a job. They will help

you analyze options for careers after graduation. In addition, they are often available to provide important personal advice.

Always make an appointment before going to see your advisor. This will assure you that you will have your advisor's undivided attention. Also, go to your advisor with a list of questions.

You can delay your graduation if you miss a course that isn't offered every semester, especially if it's required (a prerequisite) before taking other courses you need. Have your advisor review your program periodically to see that you are on track for graduation.

Adult College Students Ought to Know:

24. about the **value of remedial and developmental courses**. Too often adult students avoid remedial or developmental courses for fear that these courses will delay graduation. In reality, these courses can speed graduation because they not only provide students skills to pass future courses, but they provide skills so that students succeed academically. If you are advised to take such courses, realize that you are being given an opportunity to do your very best in school.

Adult College Students Ought to Know:

25. and understand how **students are classified** at their institutions. Classification indicates the level of progress you have made toward your degree. Typically, undergraduates are classified as freshmen until they have earned 24 semester hours. They are classified as sophomores when they have earned between 25 and 59 hours. Students become juniors when they have earned 60 hours. Once you are classified as a senior (at around 85 hours) you will remain so until graduation. Check specific classifications at your college.

Adult College Students Ought to Know:

26.   that certain courses have **corequisites or prerequisites**. A course that must be taken at the same time as another course is called a corequisite. A requirement that must be met before enrolling in particular courses is called a prerequisite. These corequisites and prerequisites are required to make sure you have the skills needed to be successful in the course. Therefore, before enrolling in any course, check to see if the course has corequisites or prerequisites.

Adult College Students Ought to Know:

27. that **each course carries a certain amount of credit** that will add to the total credits required for graduation. Generally, a course meeting one hour a week through a semester carries one semester-hour credit, a course meeting two hours a week carries two semester-hour credits, and so on. The number of courses you take may be more important than the number of credits. Four courses worth sixteen credits may be more manageable than five courses worth fifteen credits.

Approximately 120 or more credits are required for a bachelor's degree, and at least 60 credits are required for an associate degree. Colleges operating on a quarter calendar use a similar system based on quarter-hour credits, with three quarter-hour credits usually equivalent to two semester-hour credits.

Adult College Students Ought to Know:

28. how to **calculate their grade point average** (GPA). The GPA is a numerical index of overall student academic performance. It is calculated by first multiplying the number of credits earned in each completed course by the numerical value of the student's grade in that course (generally A=4, B=3, C=2, D=1, and F=0). All the resulting grade points for each course are then added, and their sum is divided by the total number of credits attempted. For example, a student who has earned "A's" in all courses will have a GPA of 4.0. Some grades will not count in the calculation of the GPA. Check to see how grades count at your institution.

Adult College Students Ought to Know:

29. that **course numbering** shows the level of course offered. Courses that are numbered in the 100's (or 1000) or 200's (or 2000) are usually freshman and sophomore level courses. Junior and senior level courses are usually in the 300's (or 3000) and 400's (or 4000). Graduate courses are typically numbered 500 (or 5000) and above. Check your registration to make sure you are not taking courses at an inappropriate level. If you take courses at too high a level, you may not have the appropriate background to succeed in the course. If you take courses at too low a level, you may not get the credit you need for graduation. Be sure to have your advisor check the courses you wish to take.

Adult College Students Ought to Know:

30. that your institution will require you to take a **certain number of hours to be considered a full-time student**. At most institutions, this number is twelve. You may be required to be a full-time student in order to receive all the services provided by the institution. Typically, full-time student status is required for student housing. Full-time status may be required for some types of financial assistance.

However, you must be careful that you don't register for a full load if you don't have the time to meet all the demands of school, home, and work. If you are working full-time, you are setting yourself up for failure if you also try to be a full-time student. If your family obligations will prevent you from devoting the hours you will need for study, you might want to attend part-time. Most faculty recommend that you plan to spend two to three hours outside class for each hour you are in class. Therefore, a twelve credit hour load equates to 24 to 36 hours of out-of-class work each week. Be realistic about your ability to handle this amount of work.

Adult College Students Ought to Know:

31. what **type of degree** you want to earn. A variety of degrees are offered by most institutions. An associate degree is a two year program of study. A bachelor's degree is a four year program of study. There are different types of bachelor's degrees. Some institutions offer specific bachelor's degrees for those majoring in nursing, fine arts, science, business. Ask your advisor or someone from the admissions office to explain the types of degrees available at your institution.

Adult College Students Ought to Know:

32. that **career counseling and job placement services** are available. Career counseling can help you decide which academic direction to take for the career you desire. Interest inventories, values assessments, career decision advice are services that career counselors can provide. Job placement services are also available to college students including resume writing support, job hunting techniques, and interviewing skill building. Look for these services at your institution.

Activity 2
Planning Your Degree

Using your school catalog, list all courses you will need to take to complete your degree each term until you complete your degree. Remember that you may need to make changes based on course availability. If you need assistance, check with your academic adivisor.

1.   List all courses that you will transfer from another institution, and/or earn through military credit or testing.

_____   _____

_____   _____

_____   _____

_____   _____

_____   _____

2. Determine during which terms you will take the remaining courses
    for your degree. (Terms 5-8 on next page.)

Term 1	Term 2	Term 3	Term 4

Term 5	Term 6	Term 7	Term 8

3

Knowing the Turf, Rules, and Players

Take a few minutes after class to have a cup of coffee with a classmate. Not only will it allow you to network and find help with your school work, you might gain a new friend that will enrich your life long after you earn your degree.

Sandra, mother of eight
One semester from graduation

Adult College Students Ought to Know:

33. that **learning the ropes**, the characteristics of fellow students who climb them, and what obstacles you'll face on the way up, will make adjusting to the task easier. Give careful consideration to the points that follow. Use them to understand how your special needs can be met as you start your climb toward your college degree.

Adult College Students Ought to Know:

34. that **asking for help is the critical first step** in enabling others to help you. When you have a problem, go to your instructor, your advisor, or the counselor at your institution who works with adult students. They not only want to help you because they have a personal commitment to see that you meet your goals—it's their job! Whenever you are facing an issue that might mean you can't continue your education or whenever you are discouraged, seek these people out. They know where students just like you go for assistance. Give them the chance to share this information with you.

Adult College Students Ought to Know:

35.   that **every student comes to campus with specific goals, fears, and misconceptions**.   Traditional age students often think that adult students have an edge over them. They mistakenly think that adult students have lots of time to study and are in bed by 9:00.   They assume that adult students will set the curve and make earning a good grade harder for everyone.   Adult students also have misconceptions about traditional students.   They assume that since traditional age students have been in a classroom more recently, they know how to study.

They think that traditional students have lots of time because they don't have to juggle school, work, and family. The truth is that non-traditional students and traditional students have lots in common. Many traditional students are single parents, having the same struggles as their adult counterparts. Most adult students work hard for their grades and have to burn the midnight oil to set the curve. Take time to get to know all students. You have strengths to share and can help each other overcome your weaknesses.

Adult College Students Ought to Know:

36. that **adult students are returning to college for a variety of reasons.** When questioned, adult students list the following three reasons for returning to college: 1) a desire for career change, 2) a change in life-style due to divorce, retirement, or company downsizing, and 3) a desire to reach a lifetime dream of completing their degree. Locate other adult students with similar goals. Having the support of those who share your dreams and goals will help you over the hurdles you face.

Adult College Students Ought to Know:

37. that feeling uncomfortable and "left out" is a **temporary phenomenon**. As you've found in joining groups in the past, assimilation is a product of time on task. Hang around after class, plan a lunch or dinner with classmates, and use e-mail to communicate with professors, fellow students and campus service offices. You'll build a direct connection to new friends and help-providers. Also find a "been there" classmate. Their adjustment experience can be helpful and a positive reinforcement for you.

Adult College Students Ought to Know:

38. that **you will know how to handle yourself** during the temporary adjustment to college. As an adult you have been required to make many adjustments in life. You know how to self-diagnose your needs and quickly seek help. Reading this book and taking good notes should help. Use this book to help you learn the following: 1) how to balance family and school, 2) how to understand about campus policies and regulations, 3) how to acquire help in tutoring, mentoring, or advisement, and 4) how to improve academic skills such as reading, notetaking, learning/teaching styles, study skills, etc.

Adult College Students Ought to Know:

39. that **your concerns are REAL**. Don't ignore them! Face up to them, and seek help. For instance, do you have trouble balancing work, family, friends, and study? Are child care concerns uppermost? Are you concerned about underdeveloped study and computer skills, lack of time management skills as applies to studying college material, difficulty feeling comfortable with younger students, difficulty in gaining support from family, spouses, friends, or employers? Or, are you experiencing difficulty in fitting into the institution's policies, procedures, customs, and practices? You may need very specific things like

more courses offered evenings, weekends, and through other non-traditional mediums (i.e. employer sponsored, community based, tele-courses, etc.). Talk to your advisor about your concerns. You may be surprised by the resources available to you.

Adult College Students Ought to Know:

40. that **your adjustment can be eased by taking a special course designed around transition to college issues**. Thousands of institutions offer required or elective short courses sometimes referred to as College Survival, Freshman Seminars, University 101, or similar titles. You are WHY these courses were designed and enrolling in them your first or second term can help you overcome many of the adjustment problems associated with starting college. Once enrolled, you'll meet others making the same transition and learn you're not alone in your feelings, attitudes, skills, or needs. Sometimes such courses are specifically reserved for adult students and topics covered are uniquely tied to managing multiple responsibilities while building success in college.

Adult College Students Ought to Know:

41. that there are **REAL and ILLUSIONARY characteristics of competition** in class. You will find a high level of competition for grades in some classes. In many cases, it is the professor who establishes this competition because the professor has a preset curve and knows that only so many students will make A's, B's, etc. In these classes, the purpose for learning is often lost in the pursuit for a grade. Learning becomes task oriented (i.e. grades) with no future purpose in mind. You,

however, realize that the only person you need to compete with is yourself. Understanding your purposes for learning will make what you're learning more valuable to you. You'll be more achievement-oriented rather than grade-oriented and have a stronger consumer orientation regarding the value of your investment of time in learning. Don't participate in the grade game and you are guaranteed to get more out of your experience.

Adult College Students Ought to Know:

42. that **learning and class success can be improved** by understanding the value of a "study partner." Like quizzing a child in spelling, you too, can get help by learning collaboratively with others. Find study partners in each class, share notes, talk about what was taught and what you read. If you must miss class, call your partner and find out what was covered. If you both have access to fax machines, fax notes from class. Learning together works. Studies prove you learn better by interacting, discussing, and helping someone else learn. Try it, it works. [Note: Recruit study partners carefully. Match your tempo.]

Adult College Students Ought to Know:

43. that you **need to balance the dream with reality**. The average grade earned in courses is a "C", not an "A." Most students earn lower grades than they want during the first term as they get readjusted to being in a school environment. Too often, these realities cause undue stress on adult students as they allow the desire for earning academic honors get in the way of enjoying the experience of being a student. Upon graduating it won't matter if you have earned a 3.0 or 4.0 GPA. Your degree, coupled with your life experiences, will be the most important factors an employer considers as you start or change careers.

Adult College Students Ought to Know:

44. that, when possible, **courses and professors should be selected with care**. Too often, adult students select courses and professors based on when a course meets rather than with information about how the course or professor will meet their needs. Of course, there will be times when you have no choice in course selection. Sometimes a course you need is offered only once during a particular term, and you are stuck with both a time and professor that might not be best for you. When you have a choice, talk to your advisor and other students about the type of professor that best meets your needs. Think about past teachers you liked. Why? Did they encourage student participation, hands-on exercises, and discussion? Were they rational,

step-by-step, and logical presenters of facts and content who tested you on your ability to memorize? Or, were they just great lecturers with a style and delivery that made it easy to learn and gave exams that allowed you to think? Search for professors like those teachers you enjoyed in the past. Honestly ask yourself: "How do I like courses to be taught—lecture, hands-on, discussion, etc.? What types of exams do I like—multiple-choice, true-false, essay? Do I like frequent unit tests or exams covering large chunks of information? Do I learn best by reading something, by seeing it, by talking about it, or by actually working with it?" When possible, select courses and professors who match your learning style. Your investment could make the difference between a full term of pleasure or drudgery.

Adult College Students Ought to Know:

45. that **difficult courses and professors are unavoidable**. There will be courses required for your major and/or graduation you would like to avoid. There will be some professors whose teaching methods won't match your learning style. When you have a term when these situations can't be avoided, consider cutting back on your hours. Don't overload your schedule when you know you will have to devote many hours to a difficult course. Perhaps take the course during a mini-session

when it is all you will be required to take. Careful planning is part of the strategy of earning a degree. You may be surprised that your perception of a professor or a course may not be the same as your classmates. You may find your experience highly productive and challenging. One adult student said it bluntly— "Dr. B is what I paid my tuition to get. This isn't high school. I'm glad I was challenged and proved I could do it."

Adult College Students Ought to Know:

46. that you are becoming **a role model** for your family, friends, or fellow employees. What you're experiencing and learning, both in content and survivorship skills, is worthy of respect . . . and you'll get it. The tone you set by prioritizing your time and study responsibilities will become a model for others to follow. Don't be surprised if others follow your lead by reading a book or magazine during your study time. Some

may wish to go to the library with you or sit in on a class, especially with a particularly thought-provoking instructor. Children may start their homework when you begin your study time. The more disciplined you become, the more they'll parallel your efforts. That way, everybody wins because everyone learns the pleasure of learning something new.

Adult College Students Ought to Know:

47. that **understanding the turf and your place in it** gives you a clearer perception of how you'll be received, helped, and nurtured on your college's campus. Displaying behaviors, attitudes, and actions that mirror these perceptions will help you gain further respect and assistance from instructors, college staff, and fellow students. Getting off to a good start will be your best investment in meeting your goals and dreams.

Activity 3
What is Important to You in Course Selection?

Put a check in the proper column that best describes your wants and desires for each item listed.

Item	Very Important	Important	Not Important
Time of Day course is offered	_____	_____	_____
Ability to establish a personal relationship with Instructor	_____	_____	_____

Item	Very Important	Important	Not Important
Instruction Delivery:			
Lecture Format	_____	_____	_____
Discussion Format	_____	_____	_____
Hands-on Format	_____	_____	_____
Self-Paced Format	_____	_____	_____
Use of visuals	_____	_____	_____
Imput from Students:			
Student Discussion	_____	_____	_____
Student Presentations	_____	_____	_____

Item	Very Important	Important	Not Important
Grading:			
Based on tests alone	_____	_____	_____
Based on student projects, no tests	_____	_____	_____
Based on combination of tests and projects	_____	_____	_____
Based on point system or percentage	_____	_____	_____
Based on pre-set curve	_____	_____	_____

Item	Very Important	Important	Not Important
Teacher Personality:			
High Energy	————	————	————
Reserve, Serious	————	————	————
Humorous, Storyteller	————	————	————
Content Driven	————	————	————
Well Organized	————	————	————
Type of Test:			
Objective Test–T/F, Multiple Choice, etc.	————	————	————
Subjective Tests–Essay, Discussion Questions	————	————	————

Item	Very Important	Important	Not Important
Outside Assistance:			
Teacher available for tutoring	_____	_____	_____
Tutoring available throught indivi-duals, labs, etc.	_____	_____	_____
Teacher generated study groups	_____	_____	_____
Student generated study groups	_____	_____	_____

Item	Very Important	Important	Not Important
Expectations:			
Expectations given at beginning of course	_____	_____	_____
Expectations flexible based on time restraints and student interests	_____	_____	_____

Now list the items you marked "Very Important." Rearrange these items in priority order with the item you consider the most important as #1. Once you complete this list, you know the characteristics you desire in a course and an instructor. Use this list when you talk to your advisor about the best course for you.

Sometimes the demands of college can seem overwhelming.

Reaching Out

E-mail and the World Wide Web are not from a Star Wars movie. They'll help connect you to the world and to campus services.

George, 40 years old
History Major

Adult College Students Ought to Know:

48. that **campus resources are available** to you. When you know what needs you have, find out what campus resources are available to help you. Get a list from your college catalog or student service bulletin. Then, reach out. Consider visiting each office. Introduce yourself and ask the staff what services are offered. You might discover that there is free tutoring available for adult students. Often writing, reading, computer, and math labs are available to assist you. Counseling, internships, adult student activity clubs, and part-time employment services may be available. Services are available and designed for you. Check them out, early!

Adult College Students Ought to Know:

49. that **campus housing is often available** for adults, single parents, or couples. Campus housing is reasonably priced, convenient to classes, and protected by campus security. This may be an opportunity you will want to consider.

Single adult students often avoid student housing because they don't want to live in the typical dorm rooms offered to students. However, other options may be available. Many residential campuses have apartment options at a cost that is much less than living off campus. Honor dorms often house more mature students who want to be in a dorm that emphasizes academics rather than partying. If your only option is a traditional dorm, find out if you can pay a little extra for a private room.

While not all schools offer housing for adult students, many have referral services to assist you to find cost effective, convenient housing options. Be sure to ask.

Adult College Students Ought to Know:

50. that many campuses **provide some type of health services** to students. These services are not restricted to students who live on campus. For the most part, only basic routine care is given. In many cases, services that aren't provided free are provided at a greatly reduced price. Visit your institution's health office. In an emergency, you'll be glad to know where it is located.

Student health insurance is sometimes available for students. This insurance can provide medical care at greatly reduced prices.

Adult College Students Ought to Know:

51. that many campuses provide a **gym or health and wellness facility** for their students. While enrolled, you can use equipment that is often found at expensive health clubs at no additional cost. Think about taking an hour each day to work on the weight machines, run on the track, or swim. Such activity will greatly reduce your stress level. Check into intramural teams. Not only are these teams a great way to keep in shape, you will make new friends.

Adult College Students Ought to Know:

52. that many schools require full-time students to have a **campus mailbox or an e-mail account** in order to communicate with students. Be sure to check to see about the policy at your institution. It will be through these methods that faculty communicate with students, information about pre-registration opportunities is announced, grades are distributed, and other important information is shared.

Adult College Students Ought to Know:

53. the **registration process** at your institution. Some institutions require students to physically register during a registration process. Other institutions allow students to register via the phone, mail or e-mail. Find out when and how you are to register. Your advisor or admission officer can provide this information.

If you must physically come to campus to register, be prepared for lines. You will encounter lines to pay fees. You will encounter lines to get books. You will encounter people who are less than polite (don't be one of them). Therefore, plan to spend the day enrolling in classes. If necessary, arrange for child care. Arrange with your boss to have the day away from work. But, be patient. Many adult students believe that if you can survive registration day, the rest of the semester is a snap. So come with a good attitude and enough time to get everything completed. After you register for the first term, you will find that the process becomes much easier and you will be able to save time and frustration. [Note: Bring a book. It's a productive reading time.]

Adult College Students Ought to Know:

54. the **important dates** for the semester. Such dates are the days for advisement, registration, dropping courses, adding courses, mid-terms, and exams. These dates are often published in the institution's bulletin, student handbook, catalog, or schedule of classes. Put these dates on a master schedule for the semester.

Adult College Students Ought to Know:

55. that you should **make copies of everything**. This includes all papers turned in to offices on campus and all major papers turned in to instructors. Campus personnel are human and they deal with hundreds of students a day. Unfortunately, in the process of dealing with all these people, things can get lost. If you have copies of your materials, you will be less frustrated if something gets lost and you can speed up the completion of your paperwork.

If you happen to be the one who has a paper lost, smile and try to be patient. After all, no one, not even you, has gone through life without making a mistake. The person who has lost your paper will appreciate your attitude and be more helpful in the future.

Adult College Students Ought to Know:

56. to always ask to **whom you are speaking** when making telephone inquiries. Write down the information you received, who told you what, and the date of the call. If confusion occurs about an issue later, you will know who gave you the information. Only being able to say that "they" or "someone" told you something, won't resolve the problem.

Adult College Students Ought to Know:

57. that many **businesses give discounts** to students. The office of Student Services can give you a listing of businesses that offer such discounts. Be sure to ask when you go to restaurants and stores if they provide student discounts. Your campus ID might be a source of savings. Learn about how to get your campus ID. This is critical.

Adult College Students Ought to Know:

58. there may be **places to buy your texts other than the campus bookstore**. Often, off-campus booksellers provide texts at greatly reduced prices. These businesses also purchase used textbooks. Check for textbook information.

Be sure to check the bulletin boards around campus for the names of other students who want to sell their texts, computers, or calculators.

Adult College Students Ought to Know:

59. that you should **check possible financial aid**, even if you think you don't qualify. You might be surprised. Financial aid may include grants, loans, and/or student work programs. Eligibility is influenced by many factors, so you may meet the criteria. You may discover that local clubs and organizations offer scholarships to adult students.

Remember, the early bird gets the worm when it comes to financial aid. As soon as you decide that you are going to college, visit the financial aid office on your campus. Complete the paperwork needed to acquire financial aid quickly and return it to the campus office. Don't forget to make a copy for your records.

Adult College Students Ought to Know:

60. that many campuses provide **special services to students who are veterans**. Such services might include funding for courses, tutoring, etc. If you feel you qualify for these services, find out if there is an office on your campus that works with veterans. Many campuses have organizations for veterans that provide support when they enter college.

Adult College Students Ought to Know:

61. that most campuses offer **special services to students who have disabilities**. If you feel you qualify, ask whom you should see on your campus. This person can help arrange appropriate services or accommodations for you.

Adult College Students Ought to Know:

62. that you should **tour the buildings** in which you will have classes before the first day of class. Find out how long it will take to walk from building to building. Learn where the bathrooms, elevators, and stairs are in each building. Take your tour when the campus isn't crowded and you aren't rushed. You will feel more comfortable on your first day if you know where to go.

Adult College Students Ought to Know:

63. the importance of having **reliable transportation**. Keep your car in good shape and just in case your best laid plans go astray, find someone who will be willing to give you a ride. As a back up plan to your back up plan, learn the bus routes. Also check out parking availability, cost, and safety. Consider a car pool of study partners who discuss classes and can quiz while commuting.

Adult College Students Ought to Know:

64. that on most campuses **a parking decal** only gives the privilege to hunt for a space. Give yourself plenty of time for the daily search for a parking place. Failure to find a parking place can cause you to be late for class and impact your academic success. Also, campus parking tickets must be paid. Graduation, transcripts, etc., can be witheld due to unpaid tickets.

Adult College Students Ought to Know:

65. that you should **create a realistic and reasonable budget**. No other problem creates as much stress, anxiety, and worry as not having enough money. As you plan to attend college, include all family members in the discussion and consider the following:

Itemize Your Expenses: Some expenses you had before attending college can be eliminated while new expenses will occur.

Itemize Your Resources: Consider the money you have on hand. Consider sources of grants, loans, scholarship and money you will earn.

Construct Your Budget: Determine time periods (as academic or calendar year) and establish a monthly/quarterly expense sheet. Review the budget to see what can be eliminated or how expenses can be cut.

Keep Careful Records. Save all receipts. In some cases, expenses may be tax deductible.

Adult College Students Ought to Know:

66. that there will **always be extras** you may not have considered in your original budget. Have a cushion so that you can afford the calculators, workbooks, study guides, etc. that your instructors recommend. Have a nest egg for the car repairs, doctor's bills, and other emergencies you weren't expecting . . . even stress reducing treats like a facial or special reward.

Adult College Students Ought to Know:

67. that you should think of attending **college as a job**. Therefore, establish hours you will attend and try to get everything done while on campus. If you have children at home, you'll find it best to stay on campus and study while your children are at day care or in school. You will find fewer distractions in the campus library than at your home. Study at home as little as possible. You will feel calmer and your family will have less resentment about time you spend studying.

Adult College Students Ought to Know:

68.   if your campus has **day care**. Campuses often offer day care at a reduced rate for students, faculty, and staff. In addition, some campus day care facilities take drop-ins on an emergency basis. One overlooked advantage of campus day care is that the curriculum of the campus day care has often been developed by the education faculty of the campus. This means that the day care your family attends will have the very best in an educational program at very little cost. Before starting school, check the rates and policies.

Some organizations provide day care free to single parents continuing their education. Check whether this is available to you.

Adult College Students Ought to Know:

69. that many institutions provide **work opportunities** for students. Check with your institution's financial aid and placement offices for work opportunities. Many campus offices have found adult workers to be excellent student workers because of the maturity and work experience they bring to the job.

There are many advantages to working on campus. One, the office personnel understand that students need to study and will allow you to study if they don't have an assignment for you. They understand if you need to rearrange your schedule so that you can study for a test. Two, the office personnel know the campus. Therefore, they will know to whom you should talk to if you have a problem or concern. Three, student workers may be able to register before other students. If this option is offered, it will allow you to register for courses that typically close early.

Other employment opportunities may include peer counseling, peer tutoring, and other peer assistance programs. Hourly wage or tuition stipends may be available. Adult learners bring tremendous experience and leadership skills to their college community and can help other students in a positive way. Plus, they can enhance their own educational skills according to the saying, "To teach is to learn."

Adult College Students Ought to Know:

70. that if you work (whether at home or in the workforce), you will need to **maintain a balance between work and school**. Most adult students find it impossible to work full-time and to go to school full-time.   Therefore, it may be necessary to attend only part-time as long as you have a full-time job. A full academic course load on most campuses is twelve hours. While this may seem like very few hours and that you would have plenty of time to work and go to school, it's important to remember that for every hour that you have in class, there will

be additional hours for reading, study, and assignments.

Often students who work are forced to choose between school and work because of a change in work hours or assignments. Talk to your instructors before deciding how to deal with this change. Sometimes an instructor is teaching the same course at another hour that might work with your schedule. Also talk with your employer about a change of hours or position which might allow study time on the job or a flexible schedule to attend classes. If changing jobs, seek out a job which would permit studying while working (i.e. receptionist, security, etc.)

Activity 4
What Campus Services Do You Need?

Put a check before the campus services you need. Then find the location, contact person, and telephone number for each service you have listed.

	Campus Services	Campus Location	Contact Person	Phone Number
__ Campus Housing	_____	_____	_____	_____
__ Health Services	_____	_____	_____	_____
__ Campus Gym	_____	_____	_____	_____

	Campus Services	Campus Location	Contact Person	Phone Number
__ Campus Post Office	_____	_____	_____	_____
__ Computer Services	_____	_____	_____	_____
__ Campus Bookstore	_____	_____	_____	_____
__ Off-Campus Bookstore	_____	_____	_____	_____
__ Financial Aid	_____	_____	_____	_____
__ Campus Day Care	_____	_____	_____	_____
__ Job Placement Office	_____	_____	_____	_____

	Campus Services	Campus Location	Contact Person	Phone Number
__ Veteran's Services	_____	_____	_____	_____
__ Disabled Services	_____	_____	_____	_____
__ Parking Services	_____	_____	_____	_____
__ Academic Advisement	_____	_____	_____	_____
__ _____	_____	_____	_____	_____
__ _____	_____	_____	_____	_____
__ _____	_____	_____	_____	_____
__ _____	_____	_____	_____	_____

Adult students must juggle many roles.

Putting First Things First

Adult students ought to know that frozen pizza won't kill your family.

Kim
35 year old freshman

Adult College Students Ought to Know:

71. the **first semester is going to be tough**. Most college graduates will say it was the toughest of all. It will take you a while to get your bearings. Don't get discouraged. You will soon have a routine, your family will have adjusted, and you will be on your way to achieving your dream.

Adult College Students Ought to Know:

72. the **importance of family support**. While gathering that support begins before applying for admission, its emphasis needs to be continued weekly. Hold family meetings periodically. Early topics include being realistic about the financial and personal sacrifices that will be necessary in order for you to attend college. Later topics would include weekly, monthly, and full term projects that everyone should understand before demands on their lives surface. Make sure everyone understands the long term benefits of the short term sacrifices.

Adult College Students Ought to Know:

73. that family members will be more comfortable about you attending college if they know where you will be each day. Plan a **family tour of the campus**. Show them the buildings and classrooms you will be using. Allow your family to have a mental picture of where you will spend your days and/or evenings.

Adult College Students Ought to Know:

74. that you need to **get your family involved**. Bring them to campus events. Have a picnic on the campus lawn. If your family feels a part of your academic experience, they will have less resentment about the time you spend away from them. Also, exposing children to college facilities can impact their futures. Studies indicate children exposed to college campuses early have a better potential to attend.

If resentment occurs, find ways to deal with it quickly. Don't ignore it. Investigate coping skills. Counselors are available.

Workshops or panel discussions hosted by seasoned adult learners may be offered. Attend. If you feel guilty, abused, or question whether you're neglecting those around you, find what has worked for others. Adjustment to change is normal. Learn how to adjust, stay focused, and help others help you.

Adult College Students Ought to Know:

75. that a great way to motivate school age children is to **do your homework with them**. Study time becomes quality time and shows children the importance of school work.

Adult College Students Ought to Know:

76. the importance of **quality time with your family**. Once a week, have an evening when everyone is together. Sit at the dinner table and share your week's experiences. Go out to eat and enjoy a movie. Take the children to the park. Everyone will have a lot to talk about and it will give everyone a dedicated time to catch up on things.

Adult College Students Ought to Know:

77. the **importance of saying "No!"** With the added burdens of school, you can't do all you did before becoming a student. It may be time to give up some activities. If you try to do all things, you won't give 100% to anything. Establish your priorities!

Adult College Students Ought to Know:

78. to **minimize distractions**. Wait until the end of the term to remodel your house or start a family project. Trying to do too many things will only frustrate you and your family.

Adult College Students Ought to Know:

79. that **no one has the right to suggest that school should come before your family**. If a faculty member, administrator, or staff person tries to suggest otherwise, remember that only you can determine what needs to be a priority for your time.

Adult College Students Ought to Know:

80. that **reliable child care is critical**. Have a backup system for emergencies. Know who you will call if your care provider is unable to take care of your child. Know what you will do if your school-age child has to miss a day of school. A missed day of school may not be critical for your second grader, but it can be the difference between passing and failing for you.

Again, find out if your campus has day care. Many male students overlook the value of campus child care. Whether you are a married or a single parent, campus child care is something you should explore. You may save time and money.

Adult College Students Ought to Know:

81. that it is critical that your child care provider or your child's school can **reach you in an emergency**. Inquire about the system on your campus for reaching students in an emergency, and make sure your child's care provider or school knows the number to reach you.

Some colleges have policies that prohibit the use of beepers or cellular phones in the classroom. Check before you use either. If you do decide to carry a beeper or cellular phone, be sure it is not set to go off in class. Remember, it is never appropriate for your beeper or cellular phone to disturb your classmates or instructors.

Adult College Students Ought to Know:

82. it's sometimes great to **encourage your "significant other" to take a course**. Even if the person you love has a degree, he/she can probably find a "fun" course to take. You can travel to campus together and spend some time alone before and after class. A quiet dinner before or after class will add to the "date."

Adult College Students Ought to Know:

83. that you should **become involved in campus activities**. Data shows that students who have some degree of involvement with their institutions tend to finish their educational goals. There are campus activities you would enjoy. In addition, you may have experience and expertise that will be helpful to your classmates.

You may never be in another situation where concerts, ball games, lecture series, and art exhibits will be provided at little or no cost. Take advantage of the things your campus has to offer that extend beyond the classroom.

Adult College Students Ought to Know:

84. that attending college provides you with a **great way to meet new friends**. You will have the opportunity to meet other adult students who share your ambitions and dreams. Many people (this author included) found their best friends sitting next to them in a college class. Invite someone to share a cup of coffee or tea at the cafeteria or campus grill. Start a study group. Get a group of fellow adult students and attend campus events together. This is a great time to expand your circle of friends.

Adult College Students Ought to Know:

85. that **you don't have to give up old friends** because you're going to college. As you make out your monthly schedule, schedule a day with your friends. The break from school and work will do you good, and it will assure you that once you graduate you will not have lost touch with people you cherish.

Adult College Students Ought to Know:

86. if your institution provides **a lounge for adult students.** Many campuses do. This is a wonderful place to relax, have a cup of coffee, listen to music from your generation, and meet other adult students. In addition, many of these lounges have lockers so that you can store your books. The price you pay to have a locker may be much less than the price you would pay to see someone about the back problems you develop carrying a heavy load of books.

Adult College Students Ought to Know:

87. the importance of **networking with other adult students**. This networking is important for two reasons. One, it will reduce the feeling that you are all alone. Sharing fears and anxieties is valuable. Two, it will give you a source of information about things you don't know. Other students know about child care, financial aid, etc. Learn from them. At many institutions, adult students have formed co-ops so they can share books, rides, skills (such as typing or fixing a car), and child care. Trading child care, cooking, or yard responsibilities with another adult student may be especially helpful during weeks when papers are due or you have lots of exams.

Adult College Students Ought to Know:

88. that **networking with traditional students, faculty, and staff** is also a wonderful part of the educational experience. Much is learned from interacting in out-of-class activities and you may find that you have assets that are desperately needed in organizations, cultural or political activities, or within the administration of the college. Never underestimate the value of networking with new people at the same time you juggle existing networks of family and friends. It helps alleviate guilt and is a building block for where you want to go.

Adult College Students Ought to Know:

89. that—ibid, ditto, and "say that again"—**the first term is going to be tough**. By helping yourself adjust and using resources and services available to you, you'll find time to learn and study. Start early. Communicate with everyone. Things will get easier, sooner than you might think!

Activity 5
Learning to Juggle Family, Friends, School, and Work

Step One: Using a monthly calendar with blocks large enough to write in, fill in the following:

1. All family activities that are planned for the month. This should include ball games, after-school activities for your children, meetings at school, activities with spouse or significant other, and other predetermined activities.

2. All school assignments for the month. Take each course syllabus and pencil in all due dates for papers, exams, projects, etc.

3.   All work related dates. Do you have major deadlines this month?
      Are there work projects due?

4.   All activities you have planned with friends.

Note: You may want to use a different color pen or ink for each
category.

Step Two: Review the calendar with the following in mind:

1.   Is there a balance in the activities you have planned for family,
      work, and school?

2.   Is there time for you to relax and rest?

3.   Were there things you wanted to do that can be put off until a
      later time?

4.   Were some weeks too crowded with deadlines? If so, what can
      be done ahead of time? What can be rescheduled?

Step Three: Did the time devoted to activities match the priorities in
your life? If not, you may need to reconsider how you plan your time
and activities.

Adult students often feel pulled between school and family.

Sinking Sounds

A. *"I'll read Psychology right after the end of the Sunday night movie."*

B. *"I'm a good typist. I don't need to learn the computer."*

C. *"Let's sit in the back of the room near the exit so we can leave early and come in late."*

Studying Smart

*Adult students ought to know that the syllabus is
only a guide. Your actual mileage may vary.*

Bernis, 56 years old
Computer Science Major

Adult College Students Ought to Know:

90. that you should designate **a place in your home as your study area**. Choose a quiet, comfortable place to study and do nothing there but study. The benefits of such action should be obvious. Humans are creatures of habit. When we sit at the kitchen table, we immediately think of food. When we lie on our beds, our eyes grow heavy and sleep becomes easier. Therefore, when we choose a place to study and do nothing but study in that area, we will send a message to ourselves and our families that it's time for us to study.

Adult College Students Ought to Know:

91. that you must **plan for the unplanned**. Think ahead to the types of emergencies that will cause you difficulties. Now, without the push of a crisis to cloud your thinking, consider the best plan to handle these emergencies. Plan through them and make notes. Then when you receive the call that your child is sick or when the car breaks down, you have an alternate plan already in mind. By having alternate plans with built-in flexibility, you can respond to a stressful situation without compounding it with anxiety over what has to be done.

Adult College Students Ought to Know:

92. that **you will receive a syllabus** from most instructors the first day of class. The syllabus contains the guidelines for the course. It describes the content and goals. It will provide the name of the text to be used. Typically it provides a tentative schedule for the term. Keep your syllabus. Some instructors will not announce test dates if these dates are outlined in the syllabus. By the way, the plural of the word, syllabus, is syllabi.

Adult College Students Ought to Know:

93. that you should **keep up with the reading** assigned for each course. Reading before the lectures helps you connect the classroom material to the textbook. If you run out of time, scan. Use post-it notes to mark material in your book that was lectured on by the instructor. This information should be given extra attention as you study for a test.

Many students literally color their textbooks by using a variety of highlighters. If all you are doing is turning the white pages of your text from white to blue, yellow, and green, you have accomplished little. The purpose of a highlighter is in its name. It is meant to highlight major ideas, key words, etc. If you are highlighting over 20% of the written text, you are not identifying the important ideas.

Adult College Students Ought to Know:

94. the **advantages and disadvantages of audio taping** a class. While an audio tape should never be used to replace written notes, it can be useful to supplement your notes. Star places in your lecture notes where you feel you need to go back and listen to the audio tape for clarification. If you have a long commute to and from school, play the audio tape in the car. After listening to the lecture again, you will find study time lessened. You can even listen to the audio tape while you do household chores. However, remember that it is never appropriate to audio tape a lecture without the instructor's permission. Always ask.

Adult College Students Ought to Know:

95. the **importance of always practicing good time management**. In fact, effective time management is often the difference between successful students and those who fail. Your time management should focus on three major areas of time - the term, the week, and each day.

Purchase or create a large calendar that will cover the entire school term and put it in a prominent place in your home. Many adult students suggest the refrigerator as the best place to display this calendar. At the beginning of the term, list all family events that will need your attention. Then, using the information found in your syllabi and campus calendar, write in all dates for tests and assignments. Add to the calendar as the term continues. This calendar will give you a quick view of critical periods during the term. If you have two tests and a major paper due one week, you will know to plan family activities for another time. Use different color markers to designate types of activities.

You will also need to keep a daily planner and a daily to-do

list. Research has shown that a to-do list is the common de-
nominator of all successful people. Find a time each day when
you can compose your to-do list. Making the list is not enough.
Setting priorities is just as important as making the list. Once
the list is made, each item should be placed in an "A,B,C" priority system. Follow through with the priorities as you have assigned them.

Adult College Students Ought to Know:

96. the **importance of the effective use of transition time**. We all have snatches of time each day when we are waiting for one activity to end or another to begin. This is the time between classes or the time we spend waiting to see our child's doctor. Use this time wisely. Always have material to study with you. The ten minutes you use to scan a chapter or review your notes while waiting in a doctor's office will be ten minutes you have for other activities later. Lunch periods at work are great. An apple and a sandwich can help you get 30-45 minutes of reading or review done. In five days, that adds up.

Adult College Students Ought to Know:

97. the **importance of stopping and asking**, "what is the best use of my time right now?" The answer may be that cuddling your child or snuggling with your spouse is the most important thing you need to do. The answer may be that you need to let the dishes soak or the grass go unmowed while you type a research paper. Ask the question, give an honest answer, and then forget the other things that aren't as important.

Adult College Students Ought to Know:

98. how to **manage big projects**. A common cause of procrastination is that a task looks so big, we continue to put it off until we have a large block of time. Reality is that you will probably never find that block of time. Therefore, when given a major project, such as a research paper, you should break the task down into smaller pieces. For example, the first step in doing a research paper might be to go to the library to determine what references are available. Instead of having "work on research paper" on your to-do list, write "check on references in library." You now have a specific goal and one that can be handled in a limited amount of time. Once you have your references, you are ready for step two.

Adult College Students Ought to Know:

99. the importance of being **computer literate**. Word processing is an important skill for all college students. Many instructors will not accept papers if they aren't typed. If you type your own work, you control every aspect, every detail. You can edit and revise at will. It will make completing assignments easier.

In addition to word processing, learning to use e-mail or the internet is critical for college students. E-mail is an excellent way to keep in touch with your instructors, friends, and family members. Many professors allow students to take exams via the computer. The internet is a wonderful way to do research for papers and projects. In addition, computer accounts may be considered part of your registration cost. Don't overlook this valuable asset.

Learning to use a computer will be a valuable skill for the remainder of your life. You will find it extremely important as you earn your degree and start your new career. If you are fearful of computer equipment, seek out a lab on your campus and ask for help. Most labs have student workers who will be willing to show you the basics.

Adult College Students Ought to Know:

100. that **libraries have changed** a great deal since you were last in school. Arrange for a tour. Instead of using a card library, most libraries have on-line services for finding materials. These services often allow you to pull entire articles via the computer. Because of global connections, students are able to pull data from libraries all over the world.

Adult College Students Ought to Know:

101. that **being late to class is unacceptable** except in extreme emergencies. When a student enters late, every eye (all the other students and the instructor) is directed to the person entering. It then takes a few minutes for everyone to get back on track. Repeated patterns of tardiness will create tension between you and the instructor. Plan ahead. Plan to be in class on time.

Adult College Students Ought to Know:

102. that **missing a day of class isn't like missing a day of work**. Many students will go to work when they are sick or when they have something else they would rather do. Yet, too often, these same students will not think twice about missing a class. You should miss class only in an emergency. No one takes notes the way you do. No one hears the instructor the same way you do. A missed class is something that can't be reclaimed.

Know your instructor's attendance policy for each class you are taking. Some instructors count absences against your grade, others do not take attendance but test over their lecture materials. It is important to know your instructor's expectations and what it takes to be successful in each course.

Adult College Students Ought to Know:

103.   that unless it is an extreme emergency, **never bring your child to class**. If you have no other option, ask the instructor for permission before entering class with a child in tow. Frequently, your child's presence will not only be a distraction to you, but to other students and to the instructor as well. Some colleges have policies that forbid children in classes on campus. Check with your institution regarding the appropriateness of children on campus.

Adult College Students Ought to Know:

104.   that you should **read your papers aloud** before turning them in to the instructor. If it doesn't make sense to you, it won't make sense to the instructor. Ask a friend or family member to read over papers before giving them to the instructor. Since you wrote the paper, you may fail to see errors. Someone more objective will find things you have missed. Also, type with a word processing program. Not only is it easy to make corrections, many have built-in devices that correct spelling and grammar.

Adult College Students Ought to Know:

105.   the importance of **sitting in the front** of the class. Sitting in the front of the class sends a message to the instructor that you are interested. Sitting in front of the class eliminates the distractions of less interested students who want to talk and work on other things. Finally, and most importantly, sitting in front of the class puts you in a position where you can see and hear the instructor. This will allow you to not only catch every word but to observe the non-verbal clues the instructor gives about the importance of material.

Adult College Students Ought to Know:

106.   that it is **important that the instructor knows who you are**. The instructor should remember who you are because you are always in class, you are always attentive, and you always turn work in on time. Go by the instructor's office if you have a question. Become someone the instructor knows and remembers, not just a name on the roll sheet. Be positively assertive.

Adult College Students Ought to Know:

107.   that you should **never be afraid to ask a question**. No question is ever a "dumb" question. If you have a question, other students (especially more traditional age students) will probably have the same question. Therefore, your fellow students will appreciate that you had the courage to ask what they wanted to know. Don't hesitate. Remember, you have paid for the answer.

Adult College Students Ought to Know:

108. your **instructors' names, office hours and location, phone number and e-mail address**. You should also know your instructors' titles. Most instructors will tell you how they want to be addressed on the first day of class. If that doesn't happen, ask. Unless told to do so, never address an instructor by his/her first name even if the instructor does remind you of your son, your daughter, or your baby sister. Part-time and adjunct instructors may be difficult to reach so do your best to get phone numbers and e-mail addresses for them

Adult College Students Ought to Know:

109.   that you shouldn't come to class with a **"know it all" attitude** because you feel old enough to be the instructor. The person in charge of the class is the instructor. You will only lose if you try to take over.

Adult students often find it difficult to change roles and become a student again. Many find it hard to go from being in charge at work or at home to being a student and having someone else tell you what to do. You may feel that you have more practical experience than the instructor. However, you should keep an open mind. There is much to learn in a college classroom. Your instructor and your fellow classmates will all add to your current body of knowledge. Adult students are often surprised at the knowledge brought to the classroom by their more traditional classmates. You are going to school to learn, so enjoy!

Adult College Students Ought to Know:

110.   that you shouldn't take the advice in Item 109 to the extreme. If you have an opinion or experience in a topic, **don't be afraid to share** it. Just be courteous and don't dominate the class.   Think, if I were the instructor, what would I want a student to contribute to enhance my lecture?

You also have the right to be respected. If you feel an instructor or a fellow student isn't treating you in a courteous or respectful manner, don't hesitate to say something. Remember to use "I" statements—I think . . . I feel . . . disrespected. This may be unintentional on their part and they often will adjust when you communicate your feelings politely.

Adult College Students Ought to Know:

111. that students will be asked to **demonstrate their knowledge** at a variety of levels. Simply knowing facts, dates, etc., may not assure academic success. You will be asked to comprehend the information. You will be asked to apply the knowledge you have gotten. Be prepared to show your knowledge at a variety of levels. Therefore, it is important not to memorize material, but to study so that you will thoroughly understand what is presented in class.

Adult College Students Ought to Know:

112.   that you should **study as though you are preparing to take a test**. Since most of what you will be doing on a test is answering questions, you should study by answering the questions you predict will be on the exam. Turn your classroom and text notes into potential test questions and then answer the questions. Buy the study guides that come with your texts and answer the questions provided. Formulate your own questions. You might be surprised how close you come to creating a test that matches that of the instructor.

Adult College Students Ought to Know:

113. the **importance of learning or study groups**. These groups are important for three reasons:

    a. Groups increase your academic success. By comparing and contrasting course notes, covering for one another when one of you can't attend class, and generally watching out for one another's interest, group members provide a rich resource for academic success. In addition, a group provides you with multiple views on what's important. A group helps clarify what you don't understand.

b.   Groups represent multiple learning styles. In a group, another student's learning style may better match the instructor's teaching style. Discussions might clarify some points you are having trouble grasping.

c.   Groups are a source of friends. Members of groups have common goals and concerns. Group members encourage each other and don't allow small failures to become big issues. They provide important support for one another. You will probably discover that you share other interests as well. Consider being the founder of a learning or study group. Student Government Associations usually have founding rules/guidelines and can sometimes offer a budget to support club-based events.

Adult College Students Ought to Know:

114. that **failure on one test or one assignment does not equate to failure in the course**. Most instructors give several graded assignments. Calmly evaluate why you made a failing grade. Did you study the wrong material? Is there something you didn't understand? Did you make careless mistakes? Did you fail to put your answer in such a way that the instructor understood that you knew the material? If you don't understand why you missed points, go see the instructor. Most importantly, don't give up. Most students find the first test of the term to be the hardest. Remember, more students fail because they simply stop going to class or stop reading or studying than because they didn't learn the material.

Adult College Students Ought to Know:

115.   that sometimes **the best action is to withdraw** from a course. If you discover that you don't have the prerequisites to do well in a course, it may be best to take a step back and get the skills you need. If you have to miss a great deal of classes because of a family emergency, it may be best to withdraw rather than struggle through and fail. Withdrawing doesn't mean you are stopping or that you are a failure. It simply means that for now, being in a particular class is not the wisest action. However, before withdrawing, make sure that doing so does not put your continued enrollment in jeopardy. If you are receiving

financial aid or tuition assistance, check with those offices before withdrawing, as it may affect your financial aid.

Never assume you will be dropped from a course if you simply stop attending. At most institutions, instructors can't drop students from their rolls. Only the student can initiate the withdrawal process. Therefore, if you don't officially withdraw, the instructor may be forced to give you a failing grade for the term. This may not seem important until you try to re-enroll or transfer to another institution and then discover that your academic record is tarnished by these failing grades.

Adult College Students Ought to Know:

116. **not to be overzealous about withdrawing** from courses. Some students do it too often. Research your options early by talking with your academic advisor or counselor to determine the appropriate course of action. Advisors are trained to understand and help with academic problems. Options may be given such as talking with your instructor, seeking tutoring support, or possibly requesting additional time to complete course requirements. Some instructors will issue an "Incomplete" grade while you finish course requirements. Other terminology or options may be used at your institution but what's important is trained advisors are available to help. Use them.

Adult College Students Ought to Know:

117. your **attitude is the key barometer of your success**. You start like a gang buster, highly motivated and focused. You encounter course work that takes time away from things you've always enjoyed doing. Your family and friends put undue expectations on you. You can say, "Wow, is this what I've gotten myself into?" Or, you can say, "This is interesting. Difficult, yes but if it was easy, I could buy it at the mall." Always monitor your attitude. The key point is PERSIST, as creatively and imaginatively as you alone can contrive.

Adult College Students Ought to Know:

118.   that **no one ever asks** how long it took to get your degree. You decide the time table based on the busy life and responsibilities you juggle. Remember, chances are in your favor you'll succeed and graduate. The key is to have a long term committment and to be surrounded by those willing to share their time as you accomplish what you want in life. Getting started out right is a proven asset. Front load yourself with as many "things" in this book as you need. It'll make the difference between an effective transition and being doomed to failure. Which would you prefer? Start to plan now!

Adult College Students Ought to Know:

119.   to always remember, **you're an intelligent, industrious, motivated, and energetic person** who wants to make your life better for yourself and those around you. You can DO IT! Just fine-tune your tolerance and frustration levels, use the information in this book immediately, and set your course and speed so you avoid the obvious obstacles in your path.

Activity 6
Making Molehills Out of Mountains

Select a task that seems very large and still is not due for a few more weeks. Take that task and break it down into its component parts.

Example: Term paper for English 101

1. Select a topic
2. Research the topic
3. Make outline from notes
4. Make a rough draft
5. Write paper
6. Proof by self and someone else
7. Re-write final draft

Once you've broken the task down into smaller components, decide a deadline for each component. Don't think of the entire task, just concentrate on accomplishing the task by the deadline you've established. Soon you will be at the top of the mountain with a completed project in hand.

Project Title _____ Completion Date _____

Step 1. _____   _____

Step 2. _____   _____

Step 3. _____   _____

Step 4. _____   _____

Step 5. _____   _____

Step 6. _____   _____

Step 7. _____   _____

Long term goals can become a reality that everyone will enjoy forever.

Conclusion

Ultimately, *you* are in charge of your own education. College officials aren't mind readers; they need you to tell them what you need. Each year colleges and universities spend more and more money trying to fine-tune their services for adult learners but the task is overwhelming. Why? It is because adult learners are more diverse and complex when compared to traditional age students. Therefore, it is important that you tell college and university administrators what you and other adult students need to adjust, persist, and graduate from college. By verbalizing your needs, you will enhance your own educational experience and the experiences of those that follow you.

Now that you've read this book, the real work starts. It is time to effectively manage your dream of earning a degree. Sure it will be tough and there will be days you will want to give up. There will be times when it will require adjustments by you and those that love you. Your advantage is your adjustment skills may be more advanced and mature than traditional age students. Conversely, you have more responsibility that needs to be carried along with you during this adjustment. You will struggle daily to balance your goals and these responsibilities. Such struggles define you as a dependable adult and give you the strength to carry through with your goals.

I wish you success in your journey as many wished me success in mine, and I hope you will use the ideas in this book to promote your success. Use it as a constant reference and keep it with you in your journey through this adjustment in your life. Use the Glossary of College Terms to learn the lingo of college. You may find additional ideas in the first book in this series, *100 Things Every College Freshman Ought to Know*. While this book is written with a more traditional student frame of reference, it contains valuable advice for all students, including adult learners.

In my career as a college professor and administrator, I have had the opportunity to work with thousands of adult students. I have shared the sadness of students who had to delay their academic goals to deal with family and/or work responsibilities, and have rejoiced when they returned to complete their degrees. I have watched students struggle academically as they began their course work and joined in the celebration when they graduated with honors. I have gained strength and courage from their persistence. And because of these students, I know that long term goals can become reality when students have a vision of what they want from life. Good luck in making your dreams come true.

Dr. Carlette Hardin

P.S. My goal is to help make the college transition process easier for you and others. If you discover "things" that you think would help future students, would you let me know? An Editorial Contributions card is at the end or, as you perfect your e-mail skills, forward to Cambridges@aol.com. THANKS.

Glossary of College Terms

Accreditation. Recognition by an accrediting organization of a college, university, or a study program, for meeting specified minimum standards of quality in its instruction, staffing, facilities, financial stability, and policies.

Achievement or Assessment Tests. Tests in specific college preparatory subjects. Required by some colleges for admission and used also in course placement.

Adjunct Faculty. Visiting or part-time instructors.

Admission. Acceptance of a student for enrollment to a college or a specific degree program.

Advance Registration . Period of advance registration in which students can drop off or mail-in completed (signed by an advisor) registration tickets to the Registrar's Office.

Advising. The offering of advice, opinion, or instruction given to students, usually by an assigned advisor. Career, academic, financial aid are the most common types involving adult students.

Alumnus and (Alumni, pl.). A graduate from a school or college.

Associate degree. The degree granted by a college or for completion of a study program normally taking two years of full-time study (or longer, in part-time study).

Audit. To take a course without credit. Student is not required to take an exam nor submit work for review.

Baccalaureate or Bachelor's degree. A degree granted for completing a course of study usually requiring 120-128 semester credits, (often called a 4-year degree program).

Bursar. The administrator responsible for billings and collections of tuition and fees.

Career services office or center. A college office or department providing services to assist students in choosing careers, in developing skills in searching and qualifying for jobs, and in actually finding and obtaining jobs. The office provides listings of job openings and interviews with corporate and government recruiters visiting the campus. Such an office might also be identified as a placement bureau, student placement office, or career resources center.

Certificate. A credential issued by the college or university in recognition of completion of curriculum other than one leading to a degree or diploma.

Challenge examinations. Examinations offered by a college that are prepared in specific subjects by its own faculty members and that enable students to earn credits by passing the examinations instead of attending class sessions.

Closed sections. A section or course that has been filled to capacity; no further registrations will be accepted without signed permission by the instructor.

Commencement. The graduation ceremonies held at the end of the term at which time associate and bachelor degrees are awarded by the university.

Concentration. A particular emphasis within a major area.

Correspondence study course. A course for which the student registers and receives and sends course materials by mail, and in which the student learns independently without class attendance. Before enrolling in such courses, students should check to make sure the credits will be accepted by their institutions.

Course. A specific subject of study.

Curriculum. The formal education requirements necessary to qualify for a degree, diploma, or certificate.

Dean's List. The published list of undergraduate students who have achieved an honors grade average (3.5 or higher) for the semester.

Department. A unit of the school's faculty organized to provide courses of study in a specific discipline such as English, Biology or Computer Science.

Discipline. An area of study representing a branch of knowledge, such as mathematics.

Distance Education. Learners in remote locations meet at a site that has cable or satellite receivers, phone lines, and video cameras so that one or two-way video contact is provided with an instructor.

Division. A group of related academic disciplines, such as the social sciences; the arts and the humanities; and the biological and physical science.

Drop. To cancel one's registration for a particular course. An option available only during a specific time frame after the semester begins.

Elective course. A course that a student takes by choice as distinguished from a course specifically required for a degree.

Electronic registration. Course registration via the computer or telephone.

External degree program. A study program or set of study programs offered by a college in which a student can earn a degree with little or no attendance at the college (often, through some combination of credit by examination, transfer credit, experiential learning credit, independent study, and credit for prior course work outside colleges).

Federal Direct Subsidized and Unsubsidized Consolidation Loans. A federally sponsored program of financial aid in which students may take out loans for college costs at subsidized interest rates, and for which financial need is an eligibility requirement.

Federal Pell Grant. Pell Grants are awarded only to undergraduate students who have not earned a bachelor's or professional degree. Unlike a loan, a Pell Grant doesn't have to be repaid.

Federal Perkins Loans. A low-interest loan for both undergraduate and graduate students with exceptional financial need. The loan is made with government funds with a share contributed by the school. This loan must be repaid.

Federal Supplemental Educational Opportunity Grants. A Federal Supplemental Educational Opportunity Grant is for undergraduates with exceptional financial need. An FSEOG doesn't have to be paid back.

Federal Work-Study (FWS). A federally sponsored financial aid program that provides jobs for students with demonstrated financial need.

Financial need. The difference between what the student and her/his spouse (or parents) can afford to spend toward the student's college costs and the total of those costs, as computed in the need analysis systems used by colleges and other aid sponsors. In those systems, colleges and other sponsors require aid applicants to complete family financial information collection forms to provide basic data for the computations.

Free Application for Federal Student Aid (FAFSA). A form that may be used by students applying for federally sponsored financial aid for college students, chiefly Pell Grants and Guaranteed Student Loans.

General Education Courses. Courses designed to help students discover the relatedness of knowledge and acquire a core of information, attitudes and capabilities basic to their formal college education and their continuing education throughout life.

Graduate Student. A student who has received a bachelor's degree and has met all criteria for admission into the Graduate School.

Graduate study program, graduate degree. A study program for which a bachelor's degree or the equivalent is usually required for admission; a degree earned through a graduate study program.

Incomplete. A grade given by the instructors to indicate a student is in good standing but could not finish the class because of circumstances beyond his/her control. A grade of incomplete is only an option if the instructor agrees to assign it and must be removed within a period of time established by the institution.

Independent Study. A program that does not require class attendance for degree credit. The student learns independently under the supervision of a faculty member.

Interdisciplinary Courses. Those which deal with two or more academic subjects/disciplines (i.e., psychology and education).

Liberal Arts. The broad scope of academic disciplines consisting of the humanities, the social sciences, and the natural sciences.

Lower-Division Courses. Introductory courses usually taken during the first two years of college study.

Major. The subject or career field that serves as the area of concentration in the student's study program for a degree. For a bachelor's degree, students must commonly earn about one-fourth of their credits in the major.

Matriculated Student.   An enrolled student who has been accepted through the Admissions Office as a degree candidate.

Mid-Term. The halfway point of a semester.

Minor. A secondary concentration in a specific discipline or field of study, usually requiring about half the number of credits required for a major.

Ombudsperson. The administrative officer at some colleges whose major duties are to receive and rectify grievances reported by students.

Orientation. Activities and programs designed to help the new student become acquainted with the university.

Pass-Fail Option. A provision allowing students to take a course on a pass or fail basis, rather than receiving a letter grade. PASS-FAIL is then excluded in computing a student's grade-point average (GPA). Students should always check with their advisor when considering the P/F option.

Permanent Record. The card on which the Registrar lists all of a student's courses, semester hours credited, grades, status, and certain personal information.

Placement Tests. Tests given by College departments which determine a student's level of proficiency in a particular subject area. These tests are used to place students in classes at the appropriate level for their abilities.

Probation (Academic). When a student's GPA falls below 2.0 for a given semester or his/her cumulative GPA is below 2.0, a conditional status will be given to the student; academic probation should be considered a warning as well as an opportunity to improve.

Proficiency Examination Program (PEP). A program of examinations in undergraduate college subjects widely used by colleges to award degree credit to students by examination, and offered by the American College Testing Program.

Quarter Hours. The unit of credit used by schools on quarter term plans.

Registrar. The college administrator responsible for supervising course enrollment, academic recording, and certification.

Registration. The process by which the student chooses, enrolls in, and pays for course sessions for the term: also, the period of several days before the term opening designated by the college for carrying out that process.

Requirements. (1) For a college degree, the amounts and kinds of study stipulated by the college as necessary in order to qualify for that degree. (2) For college admission, the documents, test results, and possibly minimum qualifications and interview, stipulated by the college as necessary in order to qualify for admission.

Schedule. The courses for which a student is enrolled during a semester or summer term.

Schedule Adjustment Days. During the first week of classes, students are permitted to modify their schedule (dropping or adding classes, changing class sections) without assessment or additional fees.

Semester. Half an academic year: 15-16 weeks.

Semester Hours. The unit of credit used by schools on semester plans.

Survey Course. A course designed to provide a general overview of an area of study.

Syllabus. An outline of topics to be covered by the instructor including assignments to be completed by students during a course.

Terminal study program. A study program usually offered by a two-year community college that is designed to qualify students for immediate employment upon completing the program rather than for transfer to a bachelor's degree program; many terminal programs lead to an associate degree.

Transcript. An official record of the courses taken and grades earned by a student throughout high school or in one or more colleges.

Transfer. Admission to a new school with acceptance of previously earned credits toward the degree, diploma, certificate, or program requirements of the new school.

Transfer Credit. Credit accepted by a college toward a degree on the basis of prior study by the student at another college.

Transfer Program. A study program usually offered by a two-year community college that is designed to qualify students completing the program for transfer to a bachelor's degree program with little or no loss of credit; most transfer programs lead to an associate degree.

Trimester. An alternate name for semester employed by colleges that offer year-round study. Three trimesters make up one year (with the third trimester representing their summer sessions).

Tuition. The amount of money charged to students for instructional services (course fees).

Undergraduate. Pertaining to studies for associate or bachelor's degrees.

Upper Division. Courses at the level of the junior and senior years of study for a bachelor's degree.

Web-based Courses. Courses offered via the Internet.

Weekend College Study Program. A study program designed especially for working adults in which students attend course sessions primarily or entirely during weekends.

Withdrawal. A release from enrollment. A student may usually withdraw from a course officially within a specified period without being graded. Withdrawal without permission may result in a failing grade.

Sources:
U.S. Department of Education Financial Aid Student Guide - 1999-2000
Various university catalogs and bulletins

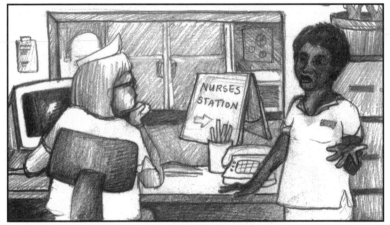

Nurse's aide, Cindy: "Is college tough?"

Nurse's aide, Sandra: "Not really! What's tough is saying 'No' to the kids, my husband, my supervisor, and telling my family I won't have Thanksgiving dinner!"

Editorial Comments and Contribution Pages

Dear Reader,

Your comments can help other adult college students make a smoother transition to college. Please share your thoughts, ideas, and suggestions on the following pages or on a separate sheet of paper. Also, fill in the biographical information below. I'll include a special reference by-line in my next edition to acknowledge all contributors. Thank you!

Name		☐ *Student*
		☐ *Faculty*
Institution		☐ *Administrator*
City	State _____ Zip _____	☐ *Family/Friend*
		☐ _____

(Cut or tear out form or e-mail to Cambridges@aol.com)

My thoughts, ideas, and suggestions are

_____

_____

_____

_____

_____

_____

_____

_____

_____

_____

_____

_____

(Cut or tear out form or e-mail to Cambridges@aol.com)

_____

_____

_____

_____

_____

_____

_____

_____

Mail To: Dr. Carlette Jackson Hardin
             c/o The Cambridge Stratford Study Skills Institute
             8560 Main Street
             Williamsville, NY 14221

(Cut or tear out form or e-mail to Cambridges@aol.com)

Phone Chat

"How's college going?"

"Oh, it's great. I'm getting very time oriented.
– I walk the dog with my head phones on playing
* Psychology 101,*
– the kids and I go to the library together,
– and when Herb complains of road rage, I simply
* say, 'How does that make you feel?'"*

Works Consulted

Apps , J. W. (1981). *The adult learner on campus*. Chicago: Follett Publishing Company.

Cross, K. P. (1976). *Accent on learning*. San Francisco: Jossey-Bass Publishers.

Disbro, W. (1995). *100 things every college freshman ought to know*. Williamsville, NY: The Cambridge Stratford Study Skills Institute.

Greenfeig, B. R., & Goldberg, B. J. (1984). Orienting returning adult students. In M. L. Upcraft (Ed.). *Orientating students to college*. San Francisco: Jossey-Bass.

Haponski, W. C., & McCabe, C. E. (1985). *The education and career planning guide for adults*. Princeton, N.J.: Peterson's Guides.

Hardin, C. J. (1987). *A college yearbook: Making it through the first year*. Lexington, MA: Ginn Press.

Knowles, M. S. (1980). *The modern practice of adult education*. New York: Cambridge.

Knowles, M. S. (1984). *Androgody in action*. San Francisco: Jossey-Bass.

Hodgkinson, H. L. (1985). *The changing face of tomorrow's student. Change, 39*, 38-39.

Mendelsohn, P. (1986). *Happier by degrees*. Berkeley: Ten Speed.

Smith, L. N., & Walter, T. L. (1992). *The mountain is high*. Belmont, CA: Wadsworth Publishing Company

UpCraft, M. L., & Gardner, J. N. (1989). *The freshman year experience*. San Francisco: Jossey-Bass.

Great Web Sites for Adults Students

http://www.collegenet.com/
        On-line College Applications and Free Financial Aid Advice

http://www.gseis.ucla.edu/mm/cc/home.html
        College Choice Web Site

http://www.ed.gov/prog_info/SFA/StudentGuide/
        Financial Aid from the U.S. Department of Education

http://www.luminet.net/~jackp/survive.html
        The Student Survival Guide

http://www.petersons.com/
        Peterson's Guide to Colleges

http:/ / www.antshe.org /
     Association for Non-Traditional Students in Higher Education

http:/ / www.csbsju.edu / academicadvising / helplist.html
     Study Skills Guides

http:/ / www.mtsu.edu / ~studskl / index.html
     Study Skills Help Page

Index by Item Number

About the Publisher
The Cambridge Stratford Study Skills Institute

Cambridge Stratford, Ltd. formed The Cambridge Stratford Study Skills Institute in 1985 with the help of its current president, Peter W. Stevens, a former vice president from a private college in New York. It is an international organization of learning and study skills specialists and tutor training professionals dedicated to helping students of all ages to STUDY SMARTER, READ FASTER and SCORE HIGHER ON TESTS, key ingredients for success in school as well as in life.

Cambridge Stratford Study Skills Course System

The CSSS INSTITUTE provides teacher and tutor training services, private courses for students in summer and after school programs nationally, and publishes the internationally renowned study skills curriculum entitled **The Cambridge Stratford Study Skills Course**. It is taught publicly by schools, colleges, federal and state grant programs at 3 levels (6–8th: 20 hour edition, 9–11th: 30 hour edition, and 12–15th: 10 hour edition, entitled *Ten Tips for Academic Success*, available in English and Spanish). These editions include 4 components; Student Workbook, Teacher Manual, Transparency and Listening Tape Set.

Tutor Training Research Study

In 1994, The INSTITUTE introduced a research-based tutor training curriculum nationally under the direction of Dr. Ross MacDonald entitled *The Master Tutor: A Guidebook for More Effective Tutoring*. It includes the state-of-the-art methods tutors can use to improve one-on-one tutoring sessions and consists of a self-instructional Guidebook for tutors, a Tutor Trainer's Manual, and Transparency Set. A pre- and post-assessment, **The TESAT** (Tutor Evaluation and Self-Assessment Tool) is available for validating improved tutoring skills.

Improving the Retention of College Students

The CSSS INSTITUTE's mission is to help students prepare for and succeed in college. This newest book, *100 Things Every Adult College Student Ought to Know*, represents its further effort to help adult college-bound students adjust to the difficult transition required in becoming a successful college student. It is a suggested reading for every adult planning to start college for the first time, as well as those who may be returning to college after a lapse in time. Colleges may find it helpful in their retention-management efforts since it helps adult students understand college customs, practices, vocabulary, and procedures, plus includes important tips for balancing responsibilities in college, family, and work environments. It is complemented by a first edition, *100 Things Every College Freshman Ought to Know*, by Professor William Disbro.

If you need information about any of the products or services offered or would like a sample lesson (PREVIEW MANUAL) forwarded for your review, write or call today.

NOTE: Prospective Authors — ***100 Things*** is being planned as a series. If you have an idea, book, or concept that might help students succeed in school or college, please contact us. We're interested!

The Cambridge Stratford Study Skills Institute
8560 Main Street
Williamsville, New York 14221
(716) 626-9044 or FAX (716) 626-9076
Cambridges@aol.com

"*Experienced travelers know that in order to get the most out of a journey, it's a good idea to consult a travel guide for information about the customs, language, and resources needed to make the most of their time and money. Dr. Hardin's **100 Things Every Adult College Student Ought to Know** provides adult students with the travel savvy necessary to make their college educational journey less rocky.*"

> Dr. Carolyn Hopper
> Study Skills Coordinator
> Middle Tennessee State University

*"**100 Things Every Adult College Student Ought to Know** provides potential and current students a useful guide as they embark upon their path to lifelong learning. By utilizing practical information and exercises, Dr. Hardin helps to eliminate the fears and apprehensions of the adult student. The diversity of information is applicable for all levels and types of education and training programs. This book is a 'must' for all adult learner programs."*

Marius "Gabe" DeGabriele
Executive Director, Association for
Non-Traditional Students in
Higher Education (ANTSHE)

*"**100 Things Every Adult College Student Ought to Know** offers adult students a compass and a navigation map for the murky waters of a college campus. It provides the vocabulary, the questions to ask, decision making assistance, and tips to enable adult students to be relieved of the fears associated with setting foot on campus.*

Having worked with adult students for a number of years as the coordinator of an adult high school, my colleagues and I often talked of how to support mature students attending school. This book is exactly what we had in mind."

Susan Simms, Ed. D.
Former Coordinator – Cohn Adult High School
Nashville, TN